JOHN ADAMS

Our Second President

AMERICAN HEROES

JOHN ADAMS
Our Second President

SNEED B. COLLARD III

Marshall Cavendish
Benchmark
New York

For Carol York, a true patriot

Marshall Cavendish Benchmark
99 White Plains Road
Tarrytown, New York 10591-9001
www.marshallcavendish.us

Text copyright © 2007 by Sneed B. Collard III

Library of Congress Cataloging-in-Publication Data
Collard, Sneed B.
John Adams : our second president / by Sneed B. Collard III.
p. cm. — (American heroes)
Summary: "A juvenile biography of John Adams, our second president"—Provided by publisher.
Includes index.
ISBN-13: 978-0-7614-2159-7
ISBN-10: 0-7614-2159-9
1. Adams, John, 1735–1826—Juvenile literature. 2. Presidents—United States—
Biography—Juvenile literature. I. Title. II. Series.
E322.C68 2006
973.44092—dc22   2005027928

Editor: Joyce Stanton
Editorial Director: Michelle Bisson
Art Director: Anahid Hamparian
Series Designer and Compositor: Anne Scatto / PIXEL PRESS
Printed in Malaysia
1 3 5 6 4 2

Images provided by Rose Corbett Gordon, Art Editor, Mystic, CT, from the following sources:
Front cover: Hulton Archive/Getty Images
Back cover: Massachusetts Historical Society, Boston/Bridgeman Art Library
Pages i, 12, 28, 32 left & right: Hulton Archive/Getty Images; *page ii, 11:* The Granger Collection; *pages vi, 23 left:* U.S. Department of the Interior, National Park Service, Adams National Historical Park; *page 1:* North Wind Picture Archive; *page 3:* Private Collection/Bridgeman Art Library; *page 4:* Bettmann/Corbis; *page 7 left & right:* Massachusetts Historical Society, Boston/Bridgeman Art Library; *pages 8, 34:* National Portrait Gallery, Smithsonian Institution/Art Resource, NY; *page 15:* Courtesy of Historical Society of Pennsylvania Collection, Atwater Kent Museum of Philadelphia/Bridgeman Art Archive; *page 16:* Art Resource, NY; *page 19:* PoodlesRock/Corbis; *page 20:* Erich Lessing/Art Resource, NY; *page 23 center & right:* Courtesy of the Massachusetts Historical Society; *page 24:* The Art Archive/Chateau de Blerancourt/Dagli Orti; *pages 27, 31:* The Art Archive/Culver Pictures.

CONTENTS

John was born in Braintree, Massachusetts, in the house on the right.
Later, he and his family lived in the house on the left.

John Adams

John Adams was the second president of the United States. He was honest and friendly. He valued hard work and education. More than anything, he valued independence. He worked hard to create the great nation we live in today.

John Adams was born in 1735. At that time, Great Britain still ruled the 13 American colonies. John grew up in the town of Braintree, Massachusetts. His childhood, he later wrote, "went off like a fairytale."

He explored the farms and beaches around his home. He flew kites, shot marbles, and went to dances with the other boys and girls of his village.

When he was ten years old, John told his father he wanted to be a farmer. His father was a farmer himself. He took his son out into a field and made him cut straw all day.

That evening, his father asked, "Well, John, are you satisfied with being a farmer?"

John replied, "I like it very well."

"Ay," his father said, "but I don't like it so well, so you shall go to school."

As a boy, John loved to explore the beaches and farms near his home.

Harvard College helped give John a love of learning.

John was a bright student. At age 16, he entered Harvard College. There, he discovered "a love of books, and a fondness for study." He joined in lively debates about religion, science, and government. He also discovered a gift for public speaking.

Not everyone liked John. Some people thought he was too proud and full of himself. Inside, John didn't feel that way. Often, he felt that he wasn't as good as other people. That's why he tried so hard at everything he did.

After college, John became a lawyer. In 1764, he married Abigail Smith. Like John, Abigail loved books. She believed in justice and honesty. She and John were best friends. Their first child, Abigail Adams, was born in 1765. Four more children followed.

John married Abigail Smith in 1764. They were best friends.

*Like his father, John Quincy Adams would one day
become president of the United States.*

John and Abigail's oldest son was John Quincy Adams. He himself would one day be president.

Now John was busier than ever. Besides being a lawyer, he ran the family farm and enjoyed his growing children. Still, he wasn't satisfied. To John, life seemed to be creeping along. He wanted to be famous! He wanted to achieve great things!

He was about to get his chance.

In 1765—about the time John's first child was born—Great Britain passed the Stamp Act. The new law forced the American colonists to pay taxes on newspapers, playing cards, and other printed paper goods. The colonists had no voice in making this law, and they were furious. Riots broke out in Boston. John was also angry. He began writing essays urging freedom from British rule. "We have a right to it," he wrote.

The Stamp Act angered most American colonists.

*Unfair British taxes and laws helped lead to the Boston Massacre—
and John's most famous court case.*

The British canceled the Stamp Act. But soon they added other taxes—on tea, paint, paper, and glass. One night in Boston, an angry mob gathered around a British government building. The mob began throwing rocks, oyster shells, and sticks at a small group of British soldiers. Suddenly, the soldiers fired their guns. Five American colonists fell dead.

Americans called the event "The Boston Massacre." They demanded that the British soldiers be punished. Only one American lawyer was brave enough to defend the soldiers. His name was John Adams.

John opposed British rule, but he believed the soldiers deserved a fair trial. In court, he argued that the British soldiers fired their guns only to defend themselves. The jury agreed with John, and the soldiers were set free. Many colonists didn't like the decision. But the trial was a victory for American justice. It also proved John Adams's honesty and fairness. It showed people that he could be trusted as a leader.

*John's defense of British soldiers proved that
he was a fair and honest man.*

The first battle in the Revolutionary War took place in Lexington, Massachusetts.

By this time, people all over the 13 colonies were talking about breaking away from British rule. In 1774, many of the colonies sent representatives to the Continental Congress in Philadelphia. John arrived to represent Massachusetts. At the meeting, John and other men began a great debate. Some argued that the colonies should remain part of Great Britain. But John urged the colonists to create their own, separate government. As trouble with Great Britain grew worse, more and more people agreed with John. Finally, in 1775, war broke out.

In 1776, the colonies voted to break away from Great Britain. They chose John Adams, Thomas Jefferson, and three other patriots to write a declaration of independence. The Declaration of Independence stated that:

- all men are created equal
- every person has the right to life, liberty, and the pursuit of happiness
- the people—not kings or other rulers— have the right to choose their own form of government.

*John Adams (dressed in red) played a key role in writing
the Declaration of Independence.*

In France, John worked to win support for the American war effort.

The colonists celebrated the Declaration of Independence. But they were still not free from Great Britain. The bloody Revolutionary War was only just beginning. And the colonists were losing!

To gain support for the war, Congress sent John Adams to Europe. In Europe, John worked to get supplies, soldiers, and naval support from France. He also traveled to the Netherlands to borrow money to pay for the war.

John's time in Europe wasn't easy. John and Abigail missed each other terribly. But John understood the importance of his work. He placed duty to his country above his own happiness. "I must study politics and war," he wrote to Abigail, "[so] my sons may have liberty to study mathematics and philosophy."

While John was in Europe, he and Abigail wrote to each other often. This is a letter from Abigail to John.

Before he went away, John gave Abigail this locket. It shows a lonely woman watching a ship sail off.

The British surrender their arms to the Americans after losing the battle at Yorktown.

On October 19, 1781, American and French troops defeated the British army in Yorktown, Virginia. Several months later, John helped write a peace treaty with Great Britain. The treaty was signed in 1783. At long last, the United States of America was a free and independent nation!

After the war, John served as the first United States minister to Great Britain. He met with King George III in person. Finally, in 1788, he sailed home. When he arrived in Boston, a huge, cheering crowd gave him a hero's welcome. Cannons fired and church bells rang. John felt overjoyed to see his friends and family. He looked forward to returning to his farm in Braintree.

But his country had other ideas for him.

When the war was over, John was presented to King George III.

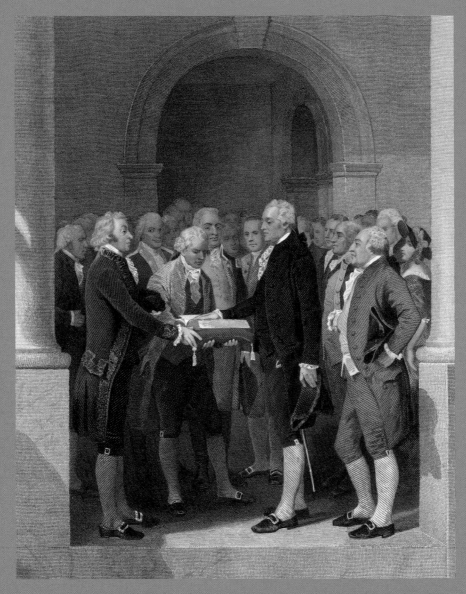

*George Washington, the first president of the United States,
takes the "oath of office." He pledges to uphold the nation's laws.
Vice president John Adams stands behind him.*

In 1789, John Adams was elected our nation's first vice president. Eight years later, John became the second president of the United States.

John wasn't a popular president. His independent spirit angered some people. Others thought he was too proud, just as they had when he was younger. But John guided our nation with skill and wisdom. He kept us out of a war in Europe. He also convinced Congress to build a strong navy. This navy helped save our nation when we again went to war with Great Britain in 1812.

John lost reelection to Thomas Jefferson in 1800. But by now, John was ready to retire from public service. He and Abigail left the new capital, Washington, DC. They returned to Massachusetts to spend the rest of their lives on their farm with their family, books, and friends.

*John and Abigail returned to their home in Massachusetts
after many years of service to their country.*

Together, John and Abigail helped create our great nation.

John Adams died at the age of 90. His friend Thomas Jefferson died on exactly the same day. The date was July 4, 1826—the fiftieth anniversary of the Declaration of Independence.

In his later years, John wrote that he was grateful for "good parents, an excellent wife, and promising children, tolerable health on the whole and competent fortune." Today, we are grateful to a man who helped build a nation based on freedom, fairness, and equality.

IMPORTANT DATES

1735 Born on October 30 in Braintree, Massachusetts, to parents John Adams and Susanna Boylston.

1755 Graduates from Harvard; gets job as a teacher.

1758 Opens his own law practice in Braintree.

1764 Marries Abigail Smith.

1765 Begins writing essays opposing British rule.

1774 Travels to Philadelphia to join the Continental Congress.

1776 Helps write the Declaration of Independence.

1778 Crosses the Atlantic Ocean to gain support from France and the Netherlands for the war against Great Britain.

1782 Helps make treaty with Britain ending the Revolutionary War.

1785 Appointed first United States minister to Great Britain.

1789 Elected first vice president of the United States.

1797 Becomes second president of the United States.

1824 John's son, John Quincy Adams, elected president.

1826 Dies at home at age 90 on Independence Day, July 4.

WORDS TO KNOW

colonist A person who lives in a colony.

colony A territory that is ruled by another country. Colonies are often far away from the country that governs them.

Continental Congress A meeting held in Philadelphia by representatives of the American colonies. At first, the representatives debated the future of the colonies and whether they should break away from Great Britain. Later, during the Revolutionary War, the Congress served as the government for the colonies.

Declaration of Independence The famous document that declared that the American colonies were free from British rule.

essay A piece of writing that expresses opinions and ideas.

independence Freedom.

minister A person who represents his or her government in a foreign country.

patriot Someone who loves his or her country and supports it with words and deeds.

representative A person who is chosen to speak or act for others.

Revolutionary War The war the American colonies fought
to win freedom from Great Britain. It lasted from 1775 to 1783.

Stamp Act A law that forced the colonists to pay a tax on many
goods that they purchased.

tax Money that people must pay the government.

TO LEARN MORE ABOUT JOHN ADAMS

WEB SITES

Grolier Online: The American Presidency
http://ap.grolier.com/browse?type=profiles#pres

Internet Public Library:
http://www.ipl.org/div/potus/jadams.html

www.whitehouse.gov/kids/presidents/johnadams.html

www.worldalmanacforkids.com/explore/presidents/adams_john.html

BOOKS

Abigail Adams by Alexandra Wallner. Holiday House, 2001.

John Adams by Muriel L. Dubois. Bridgestone Books, 2003.

John Adams (Encyclopedia of Presidents series) by Barbara Feinberg. Children's Press, 2003.

The Revolutionary John Adams by Cheryl Harness. National Geographic Books, 2003.

Young John Quincy by Cheryl Harness. Bradbury Press, 1994.

PLACES TO VISIT

The Abigail Adams Birthplace
180 Norton Street
Weymouth, Massachusetts 02188
PHONE: (781) 335-4205

Adams National Historical Park
135 Adams Street
Quincy, Massachusetts 02169-1749
PHONE: (617) 770-1175 WEB SITE: **www.nps.gov/adam**

Independence National Historical Park
143 South Third Street
Philadelphia, Pennsylvania 19106
PHONE: (215) 597-8974 WEB SITE: **www.nps.gov/inde/**

Massachusetts Historical Society
1154 Boylston Street
Boston, Massachusetts 02215-3695
PHONE: (617) 536-1608 WEB SITE: **www.masshist.org**

INDEX

Page numbers for illustrations are in boldface.

George III (England), 26, **27**
Great Britain
    Adams as first U.S. minister
       to, 26, **27**
    colonists and freedom from
       British rule, 10, 14,
       17, 18
    Revolutionary War, **16**, 17,
       21, **24**, 25
    rule over thirteen colonies, 1
    War of 1812, 29

Harvard College, **4**, 5

Jefferson, Thomas, 18, 30, 33

Massachusetts
    Adams home in Braintree,
       vi, 1, 26
    Boston homecoming for
       Adams, 26
    Boston Massacre, **12**, 13
    Boston riots, 10
    first battle in Revolutionary
       War, **16**
    representation in Continental
       Congress, 17

navy
    Revolutionary War and naval
       support from France, 21
    U.S. navy in War of 1812, 29

presidency, U.S.
    Adams as second president, 1,
       29
    Jefferson as third president, 30
    Washington as first president,
       28

Revolutionary War, **16**, 17, 21,
    24, 25

Stamp Act, 10, **11**, 13

taxes, 10, 13

vice president, Adams election
    as first, **28**, 29

War of 1812, 29
Washington, DC, 30
Washington, George, **28**

Yorktown, battle of, **24**, 25

A Note on Quotes

JOHN ADAMS left behind one of the richest collections of writings of any American president. These writings make it a pleasure to write about his life and times. Whenever possible, I've tried to include Adams's own words in this book. These quotations come from his letters, articles, and books. I found most of these quotations in books written about Adams by other authors. When comparing the same quotation as it appeared in two different books, I often noticed that certain words were spelled differently or replaced by other, similar words. In cases where I found two slightly different versions of the same quotation, I've included the version that was easiest to understand. I have taken pains, however, *not* to make up or create any fictional dialogue.

—SNEED B. COLLARD III

ABOUT THE AUTHOR

SNEED B. COLLARD III is the author of more than fifty award-winning books for young people, including *The Prairie Builders*, *One Night in the Coral Sea*, *The Deep-Sea Floor*, and the four-book SCIENCE ADVENTURES series for Marshall Cavendish Benchmark. In addition to his writing, Sneed is a popular speaker and presents widely to students, teachers, and the general public. In 2005, he received the Lud Browman Award for achievement in science writing from the University of Montana Friends of the Mansfield Library. He is also the author of several novels for young adults, including *Dog Sense* and *Fire Birds*. To learn more about Sneed, investigate his Web site at www.sneedbcollardiii.com.